Bodybuilding Science

The Formula of Hypertrophy - Optimize Training, Exercises, and Nutrition to Stimulate Maximal Muscle Growth

(Kevin P. Hunter)

Bodybuilding Science: The Formula of Hypertrophy - Optimize Training, Exercises, and Nutrition to Stimulate Maximal Muscle Growth

ISBN-13: 978-1548179175

ISBN-10: 1548179175

Contents

~

Introduction

Becoming part of bodybuilding society can be an intimidating experience for most of us even on the first visit to the gym. You see big lean, muscular men with a serious attitude training intensely. When you hear most of the vocabulary they use, at first it will seem like an alien language. Thus, you should learn everything before you set foot in your gym, not just to avoid the daunting experience, but also because you will start to train without an increased chance of injury.

Keep in mind that bodybuilding is a lot more than just oiled up muscular men flexing their muscles until they pop up. It is an art. It is perfected with sincere effort combined with months of training, dedication, and knowledge. Having the right guidance is an essential aspect since it will provide you with success without experiencing failure. Fortunately, now you already have this book.

If you truly want to have a muscular and lean body without any obstacles, this book is for you. You will expand your knowledge beyond training. First, you will learn about your body and understand more about its functioning; this will help you connect with and listen to it. You won't get any results if you work against nature.

If you search for shortcuts, you won't find them. There is no one secret or a magic pill that will help you achieve your goal. All you need to do is set realistic goals and adhere to the training and nutrition guide.

Chapter 1 – Hormones, Hormones, Hormones

First things first: you should learn how your body works before engaging in any training. Knowing its signals will help you realize the need for any special food to boost your performance. Let's start with hormones. Hormones are responsible for everything that happens--for muscle growth as well as health. It doesn't make any sense to ignore your health. Being unhealthy means less energy, little willpower, and low self-esteem. You won't have the most important motivators to push you further toward your goal.

What are hormones? Why are they important for your muscles and health? Which ones should you look out for? What happened if you have lower or higher levels? How does one boost hormones naturally? All these questions are answered without getting too much into physiological science. This book is simplified and easy to understand with even easier tips to follow.

Body and Mind Transformation: Hormones

You already know that exercise and healthy eating is fundamental to the way you look and feel. Hormones control our lives from every aspect. It affects the metabolism, body, appetite, how much you weigh, how much fat and muscle you have; and it affects energy levels, emotions, and mood.

When everything is balanced, metabolism will be improved as well as energy. This is why people who have a fast and healthy metabolism burn calories more efficiently. Those with a have slower metabolism shows extra fat on the hips and/or stomach. Burning calories faster means higher energy levels that you need for a productive day.

There are many hormones and they all work together in a system; but since I am not here to teach you biology, I am going to tell you about those that affect your muscles, weight, and health.

What are hormones?

Particular cells release hormones that affect other cells in the body. All organs create hormones; they travel through the blood and other fluids in the body. These hormones are affected by the food we eat and the lifestyle we live. Understanding which has the most effect on muscle growth and weight, and learning what food affects them, will bring you success in bodybuilding and any other type of training you might do.

At first, you might be surprised why I have started off with hormones as a top priority; but yes, they are that important. They are all about fat loss, muscle growth, and overall health. It is essential to learn everything you can about hormones in order to change your body.

There are two types of hormones: anabolic and catabolic. The anabolic builds up the body while the catabolic breaks down the body. In bodybuilding vocabulary, this means anabolic hormones help in building up muscles and catabolic means the inverse or muscle loss.

Here are the sic hormones that play the principal role in muscle growth and fat loss. I am going to explain all about their function and, most importantly, how to use them to increase your workout performance:

- Testosterone
- GH – growth hormone
- Insulin
- Thyroid hormone
- Cortisol
- Estrogen

Testosterone

Testosterone is known as the male hormone since it stimulates male characteristics. Both women and men have this hormone, just in different amounts; men have a lot more. It serves an essential role in our body in terms of bodily and sexual development, behavioral and metabolic characteristics, and a lot more.

This male hormone is produced in the testes and also the adrenal glands. After it is secreted into the blood, about 97% is bound to globulin and albumin (proteins).

This binding has three purposes:

- It serves as a storage depot or reservoir used to dispose of fluctuations in the plasma testosterone.
- It protects the testosterone from the kidneys and liver, from being degraded.
- Testosterone becomes soluble so that it can be easily transported by the blood.

The other small percentage of testosterone is not bound to the plasma and thus it is known as free testosterone. It interacts with cells and causes physical changes.

When it comes to regulation of T levels, it is controlled by two factors: the plasma protein binding capacity and the total T levels in the blood. This means that when the binding capacity increases, the free testosterone lowers. This is why certain T supplements and certain drugs can reduce its capacity and there is freer testosterone.

Even when we were embryos, T levels had the final word for us being male or female. For males, testosterone production lasts until ten weeks after birth and when puberty arrives, it stops. This is the time when the levels are through the roof. In this period, men show are surprisingly different from women looking from many angles such as body weight and muscle formation, drawing them to more aggressive sports like football. It is sad that testosterone starts to decline after 30 years of age, and by the time we turn 70-80, one-third of it is gone.

Here is how testosterone makes all the difference:

- Growth of testes, scrotum, and penis during puberty
- Enlargement of the voice box – larynx-- with the result being a deeper voice
- Formation of sperm
- Hair growth – face, chest, pubic area (and for some men the back)
- Increased skin darkness and thickness
- Increased sex drive
- Increased metabolic rate
- Increased blood volume and higher number of red blood cells
- Kidneys retain water and sodium

- Increased muscle protein, which means muscle mass is increased
- Muscle glycogen gets broken down less during exercise
- Bones retain calcium
- Sebaceous glands (sweat) are increased and in some cases result in acne
- Promotes strengthening and narrowing of the pelvis

These are just a few illustrative testosterone functions; there are many other effects on the body not listed here. I now want to inform you about the role of testosterone on bodybuilding.

Low Testosterone

Since testosterone is responsible for many functions, when decreased it can result in significant psychological and physical changes. The low limit of T in men is 300 ng/dL and the upper limit is 1000-1200 ng/dL. But how do see the first signs of low T before even getting checked? What causes low T?

Sign 1 – Sexual Function

Since testosterone decline is normal, many men worry that the time will come when sexual performance and desire will be affected. But age is not always a trigger of low T because that change happens slowly and low sex drive doesn't occur right away. However, there are three signs that your levels are too low:

- Reduced sex desire
- Less spontaneous erections, like during sleep
- Infertility

Do not mix up low T with ED (erectile dysfunction). Testosterone only plays a small role in this case. T therapy might help with ED, but it is not the cause.

Sign 2 – Physical Changes

You already know why this hormone is known as the male hormone because it gives male characteristics. It increases body hair and muscle mass, and it helps with the formation of strong and lean muscles. If testosterone is low, these physical changes can happen:

- Body fat is increased
- Decreases mass and strength of muscles

- Fragile bones
- Less body hair
- Tenderness/swelling in breast tissue
- Increased fatigue
- Hot flashes
- Cholesterol metabolism is altered

Sign 3 – Sleep Disturbances

Despite the fact that low T can cause low energy, it can also cause sleep problems like changes in sleep patterns and, in some cases, insomnia. On the other hand, testosterone therapy can cause sleep apnea, which can also disturb the sleep pattern. The overall changes in the body that lead to sleep apnea can also be the cause of low T.

Sign 4 – Emotional Changes

In addition to physical changes, levels of T affect your emotions too. This condition can lead to depression and a feeling of sadness. It can degrade one's overall sense of well-being. There are even cases where people have problems with concentration and memory and experience lower self-confidence and motivation.

Since T is the hormone that affects emotional regulation, depression is linked to many men with low T levels. This can be the result of fatigue, lower sex drive, and/or irritability.

Overall Signs and Symptoms of Low T

Physical:

- Lack of energy, fatigue
- Reduced muscle strength and mass
- Increased body fat
- Back pain
- Reduced bone density/mass, increased chance of osteoporosis (more prone to bone fracture)
- Risk of heart attack
- High cholesterol
- Refractory period is increased (increased time between sex, inability to have more frequent sex)
- Sperm count is reduced (infertility)
- Gynecomastia (male breasts)

<u>Mental:</u>

- Lower sex drive, libido is decreased
- Difficulty concentrating, brain fog
- Memory problems

<u>Emotional:</u>

- Despair, hopelessness, sadness – depression
- Ambition and motivation is decreased
- Irritability (loss of patience, increased agitation, and anger)

Increasing Your T

Whether you go only with the signs you see or you get tested for your testosterone levels (a simple blood test), there aren't any shortcuts to achieve your T goal. If you expect to get info about a magical supplement for your muscles, then you are wrong. There aren't any. The best option is your way of life. It is all about how you live. It all comes down to one simple thing, changing your diet and lifestyle long-term. If you really want to have great T levels and keep them that way, it is important to stick to your new lifestyle and be happy.

Diet

I wanted to skip all other natural ways to increase testosterone because you will be doing them with intense training. Testosterone will increase if you control stress and sleep. In other words, it is important to have a healthy lifestyle in order to get your T levels in check.

Diet is important when it comes to T production. The glands need special minerals like magnesium and zinc to get production started and the Leydig cells (in the testes) need cholesterol to create testosterone. Food such as cabbage, cauliflower, and broccoli help increase T by removing estrogen from the system. There isn't a specific diet you can follow, but you can create your own diet plan with ease. There are only a few foods to stick to:

Spinach – The best source of magnesium is spinach; not only does it increase muscle development, but it also necessary for the reproductive function in young and old, sedentary and active. Magnesium should be taken at 22mg per lb. of body weight daily. As you increasing magnesium, you will be boosting your magical T levels. So load up on leafy greens and not just spinach. Only one cup of spinach (cooked) will give you nearly half of your daily recommendation, and also it is twice what you will find in kale.

Oysters – Oysters are full of zinc, the mineral that will elevate testosterone while it boosts another important hormone—the growth factor (more about growth factor later). Trainers who take zinc supplements have shown amazing results even in the first few weeks. It has the power to increase testosterone levels as well as increase leg strength, even more than a placebo.

Eating only 6 oysters (on the half shell) will give you 33 mg zinc, which is about three times more (12mg for an adult man).

Hot Sauce – Make it HOT! The hotter the pepper or pepper sauce, the more testosterone you will have. Research has shown that the hotter you can eat it means your T levels are good. It is also known to decrease belly fat and increase the size of the sex organs. Many benefits come with simple hot sauce.

Garlic – There is a compound in garlic that triggers the luteinizing hormone. It is responsible for controlling testosterone production. Using garlic as an addition to a high protein diet can increase T production. In actuality, 500mg of onion or garlic per lb. each day will be enough to increase T levels by 300% in 20 days. Both onions and garlic contain the same chemical that releases the specific hormone responsible for starting T production. Note that fresh onion and garlic have more nutrients compared to powders.

Brazil Nuts – These nuts are special because they are rich in the trace mineral selenium. Yes, it is a trace mineral, but Brazil nuts are the best source. It has been proven that people who have trouble conceiving have also low T levels, followed by low selenium levels. Those who increased selenium got their T in check and were able to impregnate their partners.

You need 55-microgram of selenium each day and you can get about 90 mcg in one Brazil nut. So don't overeat! The upper limit for selenium intake is just 400 mcg; and if surpassed, it can cause toxicity. So, don't go too nuts.

Broccoli – This veggie is cruciferous and all types of it are rich in indoles; they are anti-cancer and boost testosterone production indirectly by releasing and flushing excess estrogen from the body. As men age, estrogen increases and testosterone decreases; indoles veggies will keep them in balance. Show that you know how to take care of your system by eating indoles, Brussels sprouts, cabbage, cauliflower or broccoli.

Eggs – The hormone boost you will get from an egg is actually from the yolk. In fact. It has been proven that vegetarians have 12% less testosterone and that a diet rich in cholesterol, mono-saturated and saturated fats will definitely improve testosterone. How is that? It is simple: cholesterol creates building blocks from which T is created.

So, you can enjoy a few eggs per week cooked in any way you want. To have a balanced diet, eggs must be on your food timetable. Keep in mind quality over quantity.

Growth Hormone

This hormone is similar to testosterone since it provides the same benefits: it decreases fat and increases muscle mass. There is no need for any special diet or changes in life to boost this hormone. All you need to do is exercise, eat healthily, and sleep well. In no time, everything will be great and you will get the boost you have been looking for.

With this hormone in check, you will be in a better mood and, of course, have more energy, which will help you train more. When everything works in sync, you will defiantly lose fat and gain muscle mass.

The growth hormone is produced while you sleep; and when you sleep less, no matter the reason (mostly stress), it will lower production of this hormone.

What do you need to naturally boost the growth hormone?

- Quality sleep every night (at least 8 hours)
- Heavy weight training
- Niacin supplements or adding food rich in niacin in your diet (1-3gr per day)
- Suppress any excessive production of insulin (limit carbs)

Insulin

The hormone secreted by the pancreas is insulin and its job is to transport glucose or blood sugar to cells, which are later burned for energy. The second and equally important function of insulin is moving amino acids for anabolic action. It is no accident that too much insulin is a fat builder.

The pancreas plays an important role here because it secretes digestive hormones and enzymes. It is located under the stomach and is connected to the small intestine.

How is insulin connected to bodybuilding? It is simple, whether you are resistant or not. A person can be less or more resistant to insulin or, in some cases, sensitive the hormone. Depending on the conditions, it can become a medical problem and an obstacle in building muscles and losing fat. The conditions include:

- Genetic predisposition
- Emotional stress
- Not enough dietary fat
- Too much sugar intake
- No exercising
- Obesity

Insulin will become and remain high when carbs are eaten in large amounts. In time, cells will adapt to carbs so they will become resistant to the function. Insulin will carry sugar to cells for energy. However, the excess not used for energy will be turned into fat.

As a result of not being able to lose fat and build muscle, many health issues can arise, such as cardiovascular disease.

Practicing intense weight lifting and training the body takes more carbs so that their ingestion controls your energy. This means more than normal carb intake is needed before and after training, about 50 grams before and about 60 grams after. Remember to keep your carbs moderate so that there won't be any remaining for fat storage.

Thyroid Hormone

The fourth important hormone for health and bodybuilding is the thyroid hormone, which is responsible for regulating body temperature; it controls the metabolism, our appetite, mood and energy levels. If it is underactive, you will start to feel tired because your metabolism is slower and your energy levels are lower.

As with any other hormone, stress can affect its normal performance. This especially happens if you are constantly under stress. In this case, the immune system won't do its work properly and the body won't be protected against viruses, for example. Once the thyroid starts to slow down, the body metabolism will start to store more calories as fat. Thus, a slower metabolism means lower energy levels.

If you are suffering from an underactive thyroid hormone, the first sign will be fatigue. I mean feeling tired all the time. (I was having problems with this hormone and it is not good). No one has the motivation and energy to exercise and even stick to a diet plan when you are often tired and neither napping nor sleeping improves it. Other symptoms are muscle and joint soreness, dry and itchy skin, slow hair growth or obvious shedding. Low thyroid levels will cause a retention of fluids and result in face or eye puffiness, and swelling of legs, feet or hands. The lower the levels of this hormone, the higher the cholesterol production. Either a low or high level can cause high blood pressure.

Improving the thyroid hormone:

- Eat food rich in iodine like shellfish, seaweed, saltwater fish, cow's milk and eggs.

- Have a few cheat days, not for you, but for your thyroid. This will allow the body to adjust to more regular food which will trick the thyroid into boosting the metabolic rate. So, up your calorie intake once every 10 days. On a cheat day, you can have 3 grams of carbs per pound and an additional 15 grams of fat.

Cortisol

Cortisol is the stress hormone that might burn body fat, which is why you might have heard that some bodybuilders deliberately over train just to increase the levels of this hormone. However, its side effects arc more negative than positive.

Among many other functions, cortisol can shrink the thymus gland, the key of immune system regulation. The immune cells will be shot down and eventually die. As a result, you are going to be more prone to illness. In addition, aside from affecting the immune system, the hormone might promote diabetes, heart disease, fat gain, and muscle wastage. To sum up, cortisol is the only hormone a bodybuilder doesn't need to achieve success.

To lower cortisol and get the success you are pursuing, you should:

- Minimize stress, avoid pointless and unnecessary arguments, and relax often.
- When you are dieting, you have to eat at least two post-workout foods that are high in sugars like fat-free sweets, cookies, etc.

- Reduce caffeine, because even one cup of coffee (200mg of caffeine) can increase cortisol by even 30% in just one hour.
- Sleep longer and deeper.
- Keep your blood sugar stable and at normal levels.
- Take supplements or consume food known to have stressbusting properties like zinc, chromium, calcium, magnesium and antioxidants. (As you can see, these are same as recommended testosterone food.)

Estrogen

Even though estrogen is known as the female hormone, it is also produced by men, but in a lot lower volume. In point of fact, estrogen is as important as testosterone. Estrogen helps in sperm production and bone maintenance. When estrogen is at higher levels in men, it can be detrimental. Excess estrogen can cause breast and prostate cancer and increase body fat.

Nature should always be in control and a male body can't function properly without estrogen. The ratio of testosterone to estrogen should be in balance. T levels should remain high, but estrogen should be kept to minimal levels.

To make sure your estrogen levels are low, always:

- Keep your body fat low because fat tissue will increase the enzyme aromatase that turns T into oestrogen. In short, the fatter a body is, the more aromatase it produces.
- You can consider taking a supplement with a natural aromatase inhibitor.
- Consume a diet rich in cabbage, cauliflower, broccoli (the same cruciferous veggies recommended to increase testosterone levels).
- Limit alcohol consumption.

As you can see, all these hormones work together and bring the same results to a bodybuilder; they help maintain energy levels, promote fat loss, and build healthy and lean muscles. All this can be kept in control with a simple new lifestyle that includes three main things: restful sleep, a stress-free life, and a healthy diet. In keeping with the food recommendation for holding your hormones in check, we are going to look at two healthy diets you can add to your new bodybuilding and healthy lifestyle regime.

Chapter 2 – Diet and Nutrition for a Healthy Bodybuilder

Dieters and people trying to lose weight are not the only ones who get hit by a new type dieting that comes each year. With so many suggestions like low-fat, low-carb, gluten-free, etc., you just can't decide if you need to focus only on protein or on a whole new diet plan.

I understand your problem; I was in your shoes once. Since I was always changing my diet, lasting results were hard to get. I was going months before I could see new muscles building up. The problem was that my body got confused and didn't know how to configure itself to take the essential nutrients and proteins it needed to stay healthy and still build muscles.

I stopped listening to people, other bodybuilders, and posts on social media about diets; rather, I started to listen to my body and undertook research to see which diet or a combination of diets would bring me closer to my targeted goal.

After intense research and one month into my new diet plan, I started to notice the results I had been searching for.

A Combination that Promises Success

The paleo diet, intermittent fasting, and soup cleansing. Yes, these three in combination will do wonders. How is this possible? It is simple; let's first see the characteristics of each diet.

1. Paleo Diet

The paleo diet is focused on eating meat, which means it is one of the best diets that will provide the best protein source. Unlike a low- or no-carb diet, the paleo diet doesn't restrict carbs, but it only focuses on natural carbs found in fruit. Even when you will need more carbs before or after training, you will be getting them from fruit and not artificial sweeteners.

The paleo diet focuses on meat and is built on the fact that our ancestors had lived about 140 000 years without any farming and their food was based on what they could catch or gather on the road. Just 10,000 years ago, when people started to settle down and form a society, farming was the practice that led us to eat grains, drink milk beyond infancy, and eat food that needed cultivation to grow.

But only 1,000 years is not enough for our genetics to get used to this type of eating, which is why we have become more obese and unhealthy whereas our hunter-gatherer's ancestors were muscular and full of energy. And so they thrived.

The paleo diet is not something difficult to remember; it is simple and amazing; delicious meals can be made. There are a few tips to follow when on this diet:

- It is a meat-based diet, but this doesn't mean that veggies are ignored. Make sure that you eat a lot of veggies with each meal. Focus on the veggies that will increase your hormones and keep them in balance so that you can get lean muscles.
- Even your first meal should be filled with fat and protein instead of carbs and grains. Instead of eating dietary cereal as your first meal of the day, eat foods

rich in protein like bacon, eggs, beef, and fish. Here is a simple casserole: take some steamed cauliflower and broccoli, shred it, add 6 eggs and some bacon, mix well and toss it in a baking pan (shallow) and bake for 30-45 minutes in a preheated oven.

- Eat until you no longer feel hungry. If you eat and stop, but you are still hungry, you will find yourself opening your fridge every second searching for something to eat.
- Make sure that the meat you will consume is grass-fed and unprocessed.
- The fish you eat should be caught in the wild
- Eggs must come from grass-fed chicken
- No more processed food
- Say goodbye to sugary drinks
- Limit alcohol (especially beer because it increases estrogen); you can have some dry wine.

2. Intermittent Fasting

This is another famous diet; it is actually more of a lifestyle. You can still stick to your old diet and just add IF. Intermittent fasting is nothing compared to starvation; it is just a period when you are not going to eat. You have chosen not to eat, which means you will be fasting.

In this fasting period, you won't be consuming food or any type of calorie drink. You are allowed only water, tea, and coffee--as much as you want.

This type of lifestyle is practiced in some traditions that are still in existence, for example, the Muslims. They fast from sunrise to sunset for 40 days each year for Ramadan.

Intermittent fasting has been proven to bring success to all those searching to lose weight and gain muscles. There are a few fasting protocols from one that lasts 14-16 hours to some that go on for 36 hours.

Not everyone can keep up the fasting that long, and neither can I. This is why I decided to combine the paleo diet and intermittent fasting that lasts 14-16 hours. I do this each day.

My last meal is at 7:00 pm and my fist meal is around 10:00 am to 1:00 pm. I go to bed at 11:00 pm, which means that about 8 hours of my fasting period has elapsed while I am sleeping. Therefore, it is the easiest protocol. 8 hours sleeping, 2-3 hours spend without food before going to bed, and the other after waking up-- very easy.

But after that my first meal (it is not breakfast, which is why I don't say breakfast) is packed with fat and protein that will help me get my energy back. I eat until I feel full; and after an hour or so, I like to have fruit to get some healthy carbs into my system, or I get some carbs from a few potatoes skin wedges.

One last thing about intermittent fasting is that it won't destroy your muscles; on the contrary, you will be building them faster and stronger.

3. Soup Cleansing

Toxins always surround us; no matter how much we try to eat healthily, the air is still polluted, and everything else is. Everything is absorbed into our bodies. This is why it is essential to clean the body at least once in 3 months (with a 1-week soup cleaning) or each month (a 2-3 days soup cleansing) or 1 day per week. It is all up to you.

When the body is full of toxins, it can't work properly and inflammation, the one thing that should help it fight injuries, will actually start to fight the body itself because all the dirt that has built up confuses it.

With one soup cleanse, it is important to eat only creamy soups that won't let the stomach use too much energy for digesting. It is all about energy here. You won't use the energy to digest, and the body will use this energy to clean itself.

Since you are following a paleo diet and practicing intermittent fasting, the best timing for soup cleansing is once a month 2-3 days, or if you can be strong and go on for 7 days only eating soup, go ahead (but at 3-month intervals). If you are new to soup cleaning, it is okay even for just one day as a start.

How to create a Bodybuilding Diet Plan

Many bodybuilder beginners and those experienced know that they need good nutrition to get their targeted look and correct muscle weight. However, even "experienced" bodybuilders don't know how to create their own meal plans and, instead, they follow an already planned diet.

Wouldn't it be easier to follow your own plan? You can add the food you like and still build muscles. It is better to plan according to your responsibilities away from bodybuilding. Of course, it is not always all about training.

If you spend all day at the gym, it doesn't mean that you will get results; it means that you are not giving your muscles a chance to rest and you don't have time to feed your body the nutrients it needs.

What nutrients do you need and how much?

Even though paleo is based on not counting calories, when it is combined with bodybuilding, it is important that you do count them. And not just total calories, but also carbs, protein, and fat.

Since I hate math (and most of you do, too), I won't be explaining how everything is calculated. Why bother with it when you can simply find a calorie calculator online. Once you decide on your calorie intake, it is time you decide about your macronutrient ratios, or Marco for short.

Marco is the combination of the 3 main nutrients that the body needs to stay healthy, energetic, and build muscles.

1. 10% carbs/50% protein/ 40% fat (most low-carb diets)
2. 50% carbs/40% protein/10% fat (not my favorite anymore, but still used by some bodybuilders)
3. 40% carbs/40% protein/20% fat

I do not agree with all the above percentages because you need to calculate the right protein intake according to your weight. This means 1g per one lb. of body weight.

1. Anti-oxidants and vitamins. Yes, vitamins are also essential for building muscles, but I do not ignore fresh veggies and fruits and get supplements instead. There are also important trace elements in veggies and fruits that you won't get in supplements. It is vital to have at least three to four pieces of fruit each day and six or more cups of veggies (the more the better). Eat colorful fruits such as grapes, prunes, and berries. When eating veggies, choose kale, red bell peppers, and spinach; and don't forget those that will increase your testosterone.

2. *Fiber* – Why is fiber important? Because it will help you lose that boring fat. The best part is that every food containing fiber is low in calories or doesn't have calories at all; and it still makes you satisfied. You will need to add legumes with veggies in order to get at least 40 grams of fiber each day.

3. *Omega-3* fatty acids – Your body needs essential fatty acids, especially because it can't produce them. It is important to get enough omega-6 and omega-3 every day. The best sources are flax, anchovies, mackerel, herring, and salmon. These essential fatty acids will not only help you gain more muscle mass, but they will keep you healthy, especially your heart. Your body needs at least 5 grams per day.

4. *Quality Protein* – Why didn't I tell you about protein first? Because the food that I already talked about in the previous points already have a great amount it. If I had added chicken before everything else, you would have ended up with more than your proper calorie daily intake and you wouldn't be getting the other important nutrients. This means that it is not all about chicken because proteins can be found everywhere. Everywhere means even in big burgers, but this is not lean protein. You have to focus on lean protein from grass-fed animals.

Okay, so, which foods have the best protein? Eggs and milk, and if you can tolerate lactose, go for the milk. Plus, keep in mind that beef is not the best protein source; even quinoa has more quality protein than beef.

5. *Good Fats* – Yes, there are fats good for your body and they should not be ignored; instead, they should be counted as important as other nutrients. Mono- and poly-saturated fats are great for you. But stick with unprocessed oils, not the liquid form. Eat olives, nuts, or avocados and get at least 10% of your calories from fats. Not long ago, cholesterol was still mistaken as a villain, but not anymore. Saturated fat should come from animals, and it should not go over 5% of your total calorie daily intake. Eggs are great for this, but you have to be very careful because, with them, you can easily exceed the recommended amount.

In case you use eggs as your protein source, it is important to eat only the white (2-3 yolks are fine). So, what is bad fat? Well, it is the oil that is fried, which all that junk and snack food has...

6. Water – Don't ever forget to drink water; our body is composed mostly of it. Without water, it won't function properly. First, it is important for detoxing the body and it is needed for chemical reactions that include muscle building, energy production, and fat burning. Just like fats, water also lubricates the joints. Water not only controls body temperature, but it also helps you control appetite. If you feel hungry even after a big meal, it might be a sign that you need more water. Water can stop cravings and increase your metabolism.

I think you get my point here. You should use your daily calorie recommendation to get all the important nutrients. The vitamins and minerals you need for your health and hormonal balance, plus protein, fats and carbs to have the energy and power to work out more, will all get the results you have been searching for. There is no point telling you exactly how many calories, proteins, carbs, and fat you should get with each meal and snack, since every person has different calorie requirements and I definitely don't accept all those exact nutrition values.

Overall, follow just these three essential steps:

1. Follow the paleo Diet

2. Add at least one day of intermittent fasting for quicker fat loss (a 16-hour fast)

3. Use a soup cleanse once a month (for1-3 days) or once every 3 months (a 7- day cleanse)

Chapter 3 – Bodybuilding Principles

I never liked following rules; and actually, I never did. The best part is that bodybuilding is not about following rules but using guidelines and principles that provide you with predictable and consistent results. The principles that I am going to tell you about go together, and you can't succeed if you choose one to follow and the other to ignore. But remember that these are not training styles. These principles might even sound lazy, silly and obvious, but a bodybuilder can't succeed if they are ignored.

Principle No.1

- Work on each body part at least once a week

It is good to train each body part at least once a week. Even people who don't train each part once per week train every five days. If you are really into getting success faster, and the right way, you must be willing to work as needed to get the desired results. When combining willingness and a good work attitude, you will start to think that more is defiantly better, and you will easily evolve in your training. Even as a beginner, you will train each part twice and even three times each week.

The problem here is that when the training frequency is increased, it will also lead to improper recovery. Don't forget that the point is to reap the benefits you get from recovering. The process of training is stimulation, recovery, and so on.

When you start your training, the hunger for more progress increases and it becomes tempting over-train. The next question arises when you should train that body part again? The true answer is once it has recovered. How long is it until it recovers from the training? It depends upon different factors that include the intensity and volume of the workout overall.

Here is a simple rule: the more damaged the muscle from the workout, the more prolonged the recovery.

When you start training, it is important to keep logs. These will help you see what actually works for you and what doesn't. One variable that your workout might need more tinkering is training frequency. No matter what training schedule you follow, it doesn't mean it will work for you 100%; that is why you need to find a balance between recuperation and frequency. This will allow you to get 100% adaptation.

In addition, you need to know the right expectations: they may include back abs and calves. Abs and calves recuperate faster than other body parts. This means that you should not expect equal results for all parts. Some will require more work than others.

Principle No.2

- *3-4 exercises for each body part*

As I mention, it is essential to find a balance between training frequency, training intensity, and training volume. This principle, and the next, will help you control volume.

Even though there are some valid times when you will be doing 1-2 exercises per part, and sometimes even five, it is not steady volume that guarantees success. Actually, you need to keep it simple and limit yourself to 3-4 exercises per body part.

In this way, you have a good variety of workouts that will ensure that each muscle gets stimulated differently, with various rep schemes, exercises, and rest intervals. I recommend going for 4 back exercises and 2 each for triceps and biceps.

Don't think of the leg as one muscle group; it is not. It is a group of muscles just like calves, hams, and quads. Don't lie to yourself by only doing 3-4 exercises for the whole lower body because in the end, you will look like an unshaped muscular big man.

To be a real bodybuilder means to work on each muscle separately, like 3-4 exercises for the quads and 3 for calves and hams. At first, it might seem a lot, especially when you see the table I will give to you later in the book; but it is not. To be a real bodybuilder, you should expect to work hard during each training session.

Principle No. 3

- Practice 3 workout sets with each exercise

I have seen and heard many people quantify training volume and training session with total sets. For me, this doesn't make sense at all; and here is why.

The warm-up sets should not be counted as part of the training volume because they don't have recuperative abilities; instead, just count the "work sets." A work set is closer to the point when you won't be able to do another rep. Any set that is less intense is just a preparatory set.

Principle No. 4

- *Strength and/or power move*

The bodybuilding goal is to enhance the physique and not always to be more powerful and strong. Going for strength and power has to be a cornerstone of bodybuilding training.

When you want to train for more power, it is important to do more work in a shorter period time. This way, the muscles develop an ability to activate or recruit a lot more muscle fiber at once.

And, yes, this will make you powerful; but it is also something unique to bodybuilders. This improved efficiency will recruit more fibers which will be stimulated and also taxed to the point of adapting; in other words, your muscles will grow larger and larger.

The muscle fibers will be increased by 10% over some period and the benefits that you get will be amazing. Implementing 3x5 (3 sets, 5 reps) on a barbell push press during your routine will make the dumbbell shoulder 3x8 reps more effective.

Power and strength are about moving faster and with heavier weights, regardless of speed. This kind of strength training brings similar benefits as power training and includes muscle fibers as well. Its effect is similar, which means it will make the other exercises a lot more effective.

Do not forget that strength training can promote hypertrophy, or enlargement of the muscles, by building new myosin and actin filaments. However, the overall effect of performing heavy and low-rep sets might not be that great when compared with TUT (time under tension), achieved from strength-training and resulting in dense-looking muscles.

If you don't care about athletic performance, practicing just one power or strength movement for each body part will give your physique a wonderful appearance.

Principle No. 5

- *For each body part, do a hypertrophy/strength exercise*

When I talk about hypertrophy/strength exercises, I mean sets/reps and exercise schemes with a hybrid goal--an increase in hypertrophy and strength. As I said before, low-rep sets will increase strength; but with less resistance and also a faster speed, the low-rep set is best to increase power.

Here the problem is that these low-rep sets won't stimulate hypertrophy to the max. This can be achieved by prolonged TUT, by inducing metabolic stress to your muscles.

When you aim for a set that will stimulate more improvement in hypertrophy and strength, it would be better to use 8-10 reps. This will allow you to use heavier weights for your hybrid goal but light enough to increase the Time Under Tension.

Keep in mind that 6 to 12 reps is okay, too, but do not end up with around 6 reps because this will compromise hypertrophy; and if it is around 12 reps, it can compromise strength.

Variety in bodybuilding is critical. If you want to choose the most successful repetition range, it is an 8-10 range.

Principle No. 6

- *Do a volumization/endurance exercise*

People who like the burn feel and maximized pump usually neglect low-rep heavy sets; and those who enjoy lifting heavier neglect a higher rep-range. More than 12 reps are good to increase endurance and this gives visual effects because of the higher sets. Training in higher reps will prolong the TUT which this will stimulate better hypotrophy.

When talking about muscle enlargement, but not muscle fiber, it is called volumization. This muscle enlargement happens due to an increase in the number and/or size of capillaries, mitochondria, sarcoplasmic reticulum enlargement, etc.

The perfect sets for volumization is an exercise with 12-20 reps; and the result is fuller-looking and rounder muscles. But keep in mind that if you want larger muscles, you need to enlarge all parts of them. Failure to do this is like leaving money on the table.

Principle No. 7

- *Isolation exercises and implement compound*

With this principle, you are going to understand which one is better for increasing muscle size: isolation exercises or compound exercises. For instance, are leg extensions or squats better for quads?

Both of them have pros and cons. It is always better to stimulate your muscles in different ways. As a result, you will get overall hypertrophy by doing each exercise rather than focusing only on isolation exercises or compounds.

As a bodybuilder, you have to know that you should not just use compound exercises. Yes, this might give you more strength, but it won't be what you are looking for in growing your muscles.

Isolation exercises are not that "functional" when talking about real applicability, but they do put the focus on the muscle you want to enhance. You will be ensuring that that muscle gets the right training stress.

Principle No. 8

- *Exercise for your weakness*

Since bodybuilding is not just about muscles and training, and it is about art, it is essential to keep aesthetics and symmetry in mind. There are many bodybuilders who get caught up working harder and start lifting heavier weights, doing more reps, etc.; in some cases doing both. However, keep in mind that improvement in bodybuilding won't come if you just increase your performance; instead, it is the result of improving appearance.

Think that you are an artist and creating an aesthetically beautiful physique. Here is how to succeed. Take a picture of yourself and then critique it like you would others. Cover you head if it makes it easier for you to be more objective. Next, categorize your body parts: underdeveloped, balanced, or dominant and use this to configure your training program and address your weaknesses.

For instance, if your back's width is your flaw, focus on exercises that are specifically designed for this area. Be methodical with the exercises because it will take some time to improve your physique.

Principle No. 9

- *First, do the important exercises*

This principle is connected with the previous one. What would happen if you chose the wrong time to do the right exercise? The effects might be nullified.

nt to work on your back in order to enhance it,
e exercise last, what will happen? Nothing! You
he strength and power to lift more weight for
ɔs to address your weakness. This means that if
ι important exercise in mind and on your
it first. Doing it when you are fatigued will
ɔortant exercise. Doing it first will reap the
ιefit.

is
he
ee
ɔu

o. 10

reps – inversely proportional

es of bodybuilding come from intuition,
ɔ to common sense. But the fact that rest and
inversely proportional is not part of it.
ιually counterintuitive.

ein
ny

ɔur
ʒth

u have done 3 reps during an exercise. When
you are letting your breathing and heart rate
. You will see that it won't take long before
to their optimal state. After all, you didn't
rning on the specific body part with a brief
ιinute, you will be able to do another set.

However, if you take a rest after 15 reps, you will need m〈
rest (about 2 minutes) before you can continue and until y〈
breathing and heart rate have returned to normal.

It is somehow strange but the perception recovery is not t〈
accurate. Even though the two BPMs are important (brea〈
per minute and beats per minute), there is something e〈
going on that you can't feel.

If fatigue is reached when doing a low-rep heavy set, i〈
because of the ATP-CP system and also failure of 〈
nervous system. This means that it will take about th〈
minutes for the components to rest and replenish before y〈
can do another set using the same intensity.

If you do a low rep, high-tension set to increase prot〈
synthesis, it is essential to perform each set by doing as m〈
reps as you can with the given weight.
Do not reduce weight because this won't duplicate y〈
performance, because the tension is what stimulates stren〈
and ultimately creates larger muscles.

Performing higher reps, but with a longer TUT, is not critical because here tension is not the primary stressor; it is the metabolic fatigue. This kind of activity will stimulate a different training stimulus. Metabolic fatigue won't lead to myosin filaments and new action. Instead, it will lead to hypertrophy of other structures like capillaries, mitochondria, reticulum, etc.

When doing heavy but low-rep sets, you should rest enough so that you can lift the maximum weight during the next set. This tension will cause the muscles to grow.

Principle No. 11

- *Volume and intensity as inversely proportional*

I have set this principle as the last because it is the most critical. If you don't follow this principle, you won't see any progress. Most bodybuilders have struggled with this one the most.

The issue here is how close you are to giving your all for a set. Some erroneously believe that you do as many reps as you can, like your life is depending on it, only then will you reach 100% intensity. When talking about volume, it refers to the number of reps, sets, and exercises performed in one workout. Thus, it means the number of sets done until you reach fatigue.

It is important to know that when you are doing all-out sets in one workout, you should do fewer overall. If not, you will be compromising the recovery frame.
You can train long or hard but you definitely can't train both hard and long.

It is always better to make steady and ongoing progress. Train smart and not hard. Use your new nutritional knowledge and the principles that will be your recipe for a successful bodybuilding lifestyle.

Chapter 4 – Bodybuilding Program

I am aware that it might sound boring in the beginning, but it should not be. Before we start looking at two types of bodybuilding programs, first you should know their benefits, which will help you decide the one best for you, according to your goals and lifestyle.

For many years in the past, trainers would have the last word on which type of training you should do, but not anymore. Now it is up to you to choose between full body and split training. You can know the right one for you by understanding their respective benefits.

Full Body Training Benefits

Benefit No. 1 Frequency – The more you stimulate your muscles, the more they will grow. You are training fresh, plus you are hitting your muscles with different stimuli by varying rep ranges, and so on. By doing full body exercises, you will hit the major muscles about three times a week. This is amazing stimulation! If you do this in combination with split training, it will be probable, practical and plausible.

Benefit No. 2 More energy with each workout – When compared with split routines, full body training will give you greater energy per each workout. This is because of a number of muscles are taxed with each session.

With a full body program, you can either:

- Eat more (no fat gain).
- After weight training, skip the 15 minutes of cardio.
- Gain mass without gaining fat.

Benefit No. 3 Greater Super-compensation – With full body training, the body will experience depletion that will lead to greater super-compensation a type of protein degradation, micro-trauma, and glycogen depletion will occur. This will leave the body in a primed state such that anabolism will start and nutrient uptake is needed. This will give your body the right nutrients it asks for.

Benefit No. 4 Better Hormone Stimulation - Working your muscles to a large degree in given session will result in higher concentrations of the anabolic hormone. This increase is short lived; however, even during that brief increase, the anabolic hormones will increase the sensitive time - the time when the body starts to consume a great amount of nutrients.

Split Training benefits

Benefit No. 1 Greater Load with less Fatigue – This happens due to two reasons. First of all, the demanding nature of full body training, despite its benefits, are calorically expensive compared to split training, and they are also more fatiguing. This is not always a good thing when done later in your program. When you reach compound movement, the load will make you suffer from general fatigue.

With a split program, there is less fatigue and a specific fatigue doesn't exist. With the antagonistic approach to the split design, it will be heightened. Finally, working for each muscle group with the heaviest load possible will increase adaption a lot faster. This means that it will have a positive effect on size and strength.

Benefit No. 2 Giving more attention to a specific muscle group – When you have about two muscles to focus on, those specific groups will get concentrated attention. This will result in specific adaption and micro-trauma. It might seem like split programs prioritize everything and full body programs prioritize nothing.

It is not that true since full body training has its own unique benefits. However, it is impossible to focus on each muscle group like you can with split programs. When you focus only on 1-2 things, it leads to quality work.

Benefit No. 3 Less prone to overtraining – Despite the full body program's benefits, this type demands more energy and for longer periods. But the split programs include an extremely high, intense quality workout in about a half-hour. You will leave the gym motivated and fresh, and you will feel that you have accomplished your targeted workout program. This is an essential benefit. If you love going to the gym, you will get better and better in your training and you will definitely accomplish your goal.

As you can see, both programs are great for everyone, even beginners. With their unique properties and benefits, each will provide different advantages. Now it is up to you to decide which is for you and up to me to give readers a simple bodybuilding program for both full body and split training.

Before Starting

Simple, short tips are best when it comes to giving information on how to start training. This goes for any type of workout program you go for.

Stretching and Warming up
Don't forget to stretch and warm-up before you start your training session. This means before any type. This will stimulate blood flow, increase joint mobility, raises the body temperature and also increase your mental and physical readiness.

You can warm up with any cardio exercise and machine (10 minutes). Also, you can opt for simple warming up exercises/stretches like body weight lunges, squat-to-stand, spider-man steps, leg swings, trench or arm circles, and so on. These won't just warm you up, but they will also increase flexibility and mobility in your joints.

In order to decrease the risk of injury and increase performance, do at least two light sets (non-fatiguing) of each exercise. This is valuable before you move on to the heavy sets. It is never wise to jump right into the heaviest set and give everything you have while you are cold.

Keep in mind that static stretching is just for flexibility but not for warming up.

Adjust the Reps and Weight

Knowing the right weight, you need to use will lead you closer to your goal. It is about applying the proper resistance. It might take about two sets and even two workouts before you get the right weight.

The advantage when working with rep range is the help you get to choose the right weight. It goes like this. If your rep range is 6-10 reps, you should reach at least 6 (the lower number). If you can't reach 6 and you reach less, it means that the weight you have chosen is too heavy. If you can reach 10 (the upper number) or more, and it feels easy, it is a sign that your chosen weight is too light and you need to increase it.

Full Body Program

The full body program that you will understand now is great for beginners and it involves activating the whole body with each workout for 3 days per week. Don't forget that in contrast to split workouts, full body workouts are a great way to start your bodybuilding lifestyle. After 6 months or so, you can start changing your workout routine and advance to a 4-5 days split programs. You have to let your body get used to training first. Don't worry, you will be seeing results soon enough, even with these starting exercises.

	Week 1	**Week 2**
Monday	Bent Over Row 3x5 Bench Press 3x5 Squat 3x5	Pull Up 3x5 Overhead Press 3x5 Deadlift 2x8
Wednesday	Pull Up 3x5 Overhead Press 3x5 Deadlift 2x8	Bent Over Row 3x5 Bench Press 3x5 Squat 3x5
Friday	Bent Over Row 3x5 Bench Press 3x5 Squat 3x5	Pull Up 3x5 Overhead Press 3x5 Deadlift 2x8

As you can see, these workouts are easy and created for the first month. This month is the time when your muscles need to get used to the weights, training, and your new routine, which usually takes about a month. After the first month, you can move to a more serious and intense workout that will definitely give you results.

The regular workout program after the first month (reserved for adaption) usually will involve about 10-12 different exercises. With each, you will be hitting the major muscle groups. Don't forget that ex. 3x15 means 3 sets of 15 reps.

Targeted Muscles	Exercise	Sets x Reps
Back	Pull downs	3 x 10
Chest	Bench presses	3 x 10
Triceps	Pushdowns	3 x 10
Shoulders	Military presses (standing)	3 x 10
Biceps	Barbell curls	3 x 10
Quadriceps	Squats	3 x 10
Lower Back	Hyperextensions	3 x 15
Calves	Standing Calf Raises	3 x 10-12
Hamstrings	Leg Curls	3x10
Abdominals	Incline Sit-ups	3 x 25

These 10 exercises with a total of 30 sets should be done at least 3 times per week. However, if you see that you are sore more than 2-3 days, you should wait until it goes away and, in some cases, reduce to 2 gym visits per week. You can do some light stretches at home, because they will help with the soreness and promote a faster recovery.

You can go on with this full body program as long as you want, of course; if you see fit, you can increase the weight. But if you choose, you can work on both types of programs--full body and split. For instance, you can go with a full body program the first three months and then start the split workout.

3-day Split Program

The first question that most beginners ask when seeing this type of workout program is: is a 3-day split really enough? Training for 3 days per week is the best starting place for any beginner since it covers all muscles and demands the required effort. These workouts will build muscle mass and help you gain strength.

The workouts I constructed below will train 2-3 muscle parts in a day and in one week, all the muscles will be covered. The following workouts require about 1 hour and 30 minutes, depending upon the time you take to rest. Just don't forget to warm up before you start training.

Day 1 – Biceps & Chest (Monday)		
Exercise	Sets	Reps
Leg Raises	4	10
Alternating Dumbbell Curls (Standing)	3	Each Arm 8-10
Incline Dumbbell Bench Press	4	8-10
Barbell Bicep Curls (Standing)	3	8-10
Flat Barbell Bench Press	4	8-10

Day 2 – Legs & Shoulders (Wednesday)		
Exercise	Sets	Reps
Abdominal Crunches	3	20
Rear Hamstring Leg Curls	3	8-10
Front Thigh Leg Curls	3	8-10
Squats	4	8-10
Lateral Shoulder Raises (Standing)	3	8-10
Dumbbell Shoulder Press (Seated)	4	8-10

Day 3 – Triceps & Back (Friday)		
Exercise	**Sets**	**Reps**
Leg Raises	4	10-15
Lat Pull Downs	4	8-10
Cable Triceps Extensions (Standing)	3	8-10
Lying Triceps Extensions	3	8-10
Dumbbell Lat Rows	4	8-10
Pull Ups	4	8-10

Chapter 5 – Understanding Muscle Groups and Exercises

Weight lifting is not an activity that you can do without being mindful. Not just bodybuilders, but athletes, trainers, and gym-goers should all understand each muscle and its functions so that the training can be done properly. Together with nutrition principles and programs, muscle knowledge is the way to reach your bodybuilding goal.

So, let's start. The muscles that you are going to work on are under 2 categories: lower and upper body muscles.

Lower Body Muscles	Upper Body Muscles
Glutes	Shoulders (Deltoids and traps)
Quads	Back (Lats, middle back, and lower back)
Hamstrings	Arms

	(Biceps, triceps, and forearms)
Calves	Chest (Major & minor pectorals)
	Abdomen Muscles

Upper Body Muscles

1. Shoulders

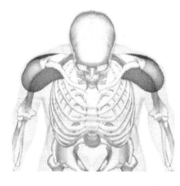

Deltoids are the muscles found on top of the shoulder and are also known as delts. Under this muscle group are anterior, middle, and posterior deltoids. These muscles aid in abduction, rotation, and flexing.

Exercises

	Dumbbell Shoulder Press
	Side Dumbbell Raise
	Dumbbell Front Rise

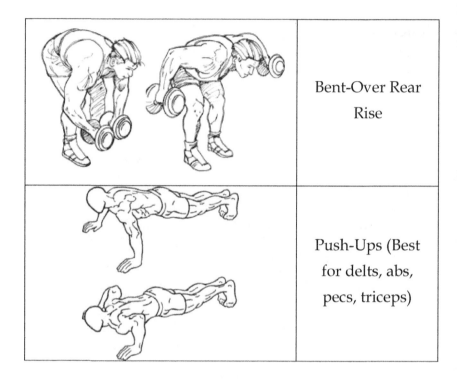

	Bent-Over Rear Rise
	Push-Ups (Best for delts, abs, pecs, triceps)

2. Back

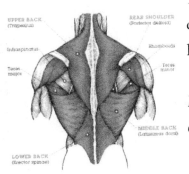

The back muscle category is divided into traps, middle back, lats, and lower back.

Lower Back – Keeps the spine and core muscles stable.

Lats – Keep your elbow close and help in pulling the back and arms down.

Middle Back – Or rhomboids provide stability for the shoulders and keeps the shoulder blades together.

Traps – The deltoids are connected with Traps or trapezius muscles; they retract and rotate the shoulder blades and support the arm's weight.

Exercises

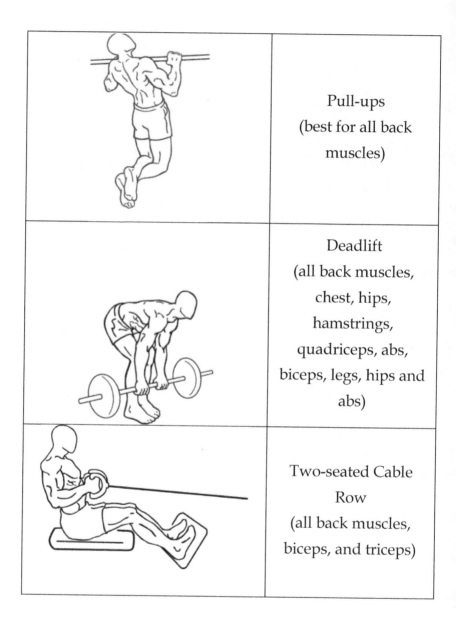

	Pull-ups (best for all back muscles)
	Deadlift (all back muscles, chest, hips, hamstrings, quadriceps, abs, biceps, legs, hips and abs)
	Two-seated Cable Row (all back muscles, biceps, and triceps)

	T-bar (middle back, biceps and shoulders)
	Dumbbell Rows – with one arm (lats, traps, and biceps)
	Dumbbell Shrugs

| | Lateral Pull Down (lats, biceps, shoulders) |
| | Grip pull-down (lats, biceps, and shoulders) |

3. Chest

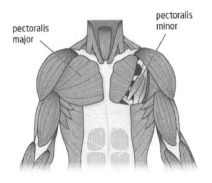

This muscle group is constructed from the major and minor pectoralis. These are the muscles that allow you to pull your arms toward you and down, and also put them ahead. Some of the exercises for the chest are mentioned in the previous tables and here are the rest of them.

Exercises

Barbell Bench Press

	Dumbbell Bench Press
	Dumbbell Flyes
	Straight-Arm Dumbbell Pullover

4. Arms

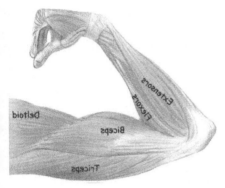

There are 3 groups of arm muscles: biceps, triceps, and forearms. These are responsible for increasing the angle of the joint and they also extends the arm. Flexors aid in flexing and decrease the angle of the joint.

Biceps Exercises

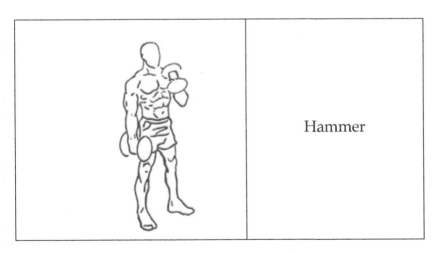

	Hammer

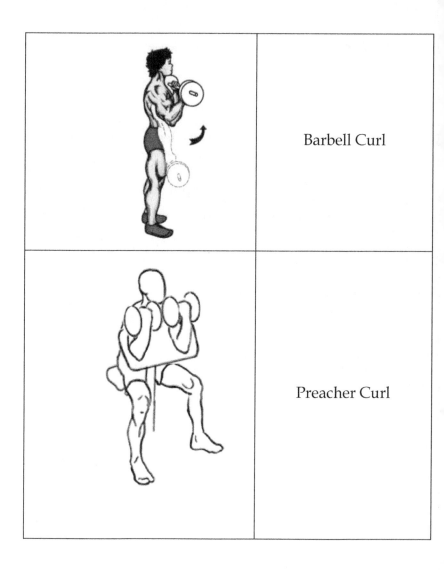

Barbell Curl

Preacher Curl

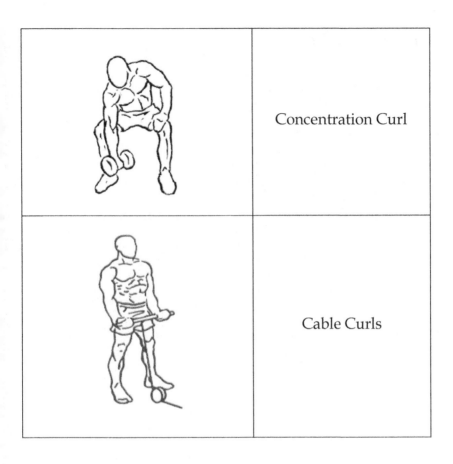

| | Concentration Curl |
| | Cable Curls |

Triceps Exercises

	Bench Dips
	Triceps Lying Extensions
	Triceps Cable Extension

	Overhead Cable Extension
	Close-grip Bench Press

Forearms Exercise

Reverse Barbell
Curls

5. Abdominal Muscles

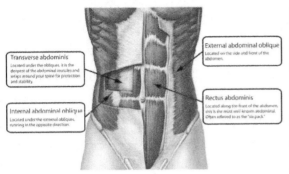

It is a fact that people at the gym usually target the abs. They are the muscle section that gets most of the attention. However, if you also want to have rock-hard abs, you have to work on them with proper exercises. They are one of the most important muscles because they hold up the whole body structure. They are divided into transverse abdominal, internal oblique, external oblique and rectus abdominals.

- The deepest muscles are transverse abdominals that support the body posture and spine.

- The internal oblique helps in rotation, bending and spine support.

- The external oblique is located on both sides and helps in rotation, bending and supporting.

- The visible muscles are called rectus abdominals and they provide body posture and give that amazing six-packs look.

Abs Exercises

Before we get to the types of exercises you must know, you must lose body fat so your abs can be seen. Everyone has them, but fat is covers them up. With the right diet from this book and a proper program with regular exercises, you will most definitely have them.

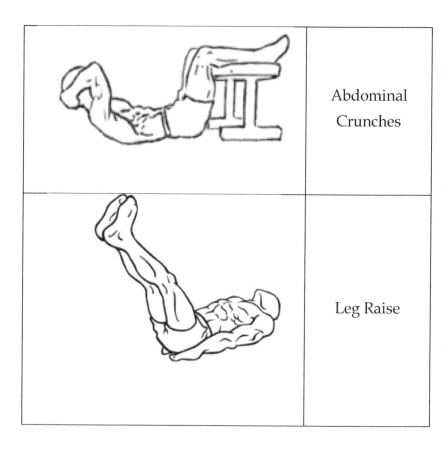	Abdominal Crunches
	Leg Raise

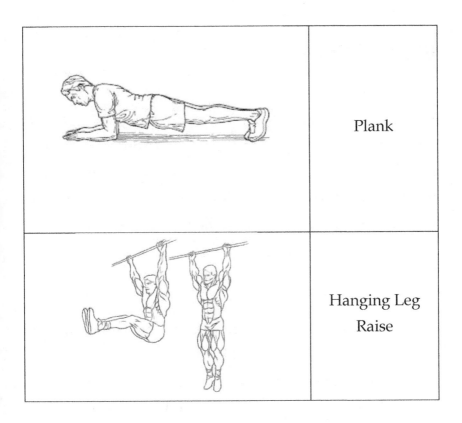	Plank
	Hanging Leg Raise

6. Lower Body

For some unexplained reason, the lower body gets less attention, which is not good. For an artistic and amazing look, and also to have strength in your lower body, this area must be worked out too. The lower body muscles are divided into glutes, quadriceps, hamstrings and calves.

- Glutes – Extend and rotate the hip and stabilize the pelvis. They are the biggest muscles.
- Quadriceps – Help in flexing the thighs and hips and also extend the leg and knee.
- Hamstrings – Aid in lower body and hip movement, stabilize the pelvis and hips, and flexes them.
- Claves – Aid in lifting the heels.

Lower Body Exercises

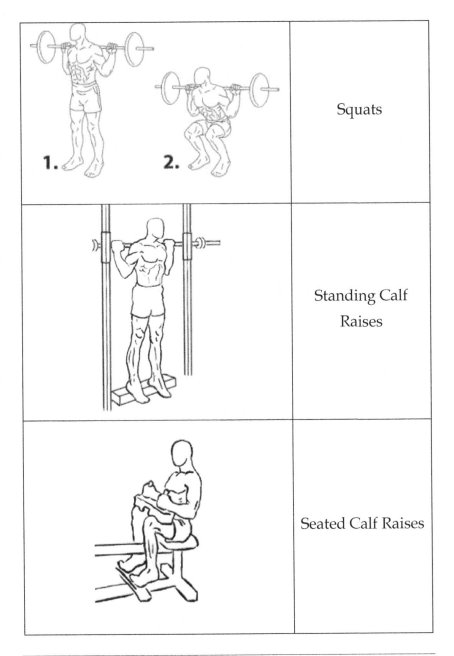

	Squats
	Standing Calf Raises
	Seated Calf Raises

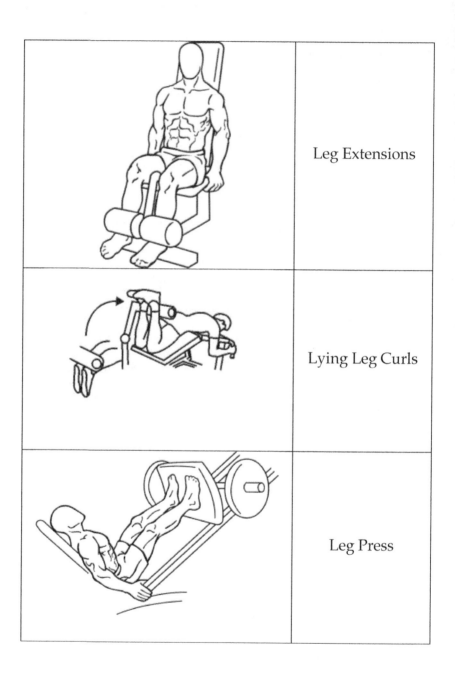

	Leg Extensions
	Lying Leg Curls
	Leg Press

Chapter 6 – Boosting Muscle Growth without Steroids

Many people shy away from starting bodybuilding just because they have heard mistruths and think it is associated with steroids. This is so not true. In fact, aside from being the most natural way to get important nutrients from food, you can get an amazing boost in muscle growth by using supplements and boosters that are not steroids. Few people know that natural supplements are great for increasing your success without any life threatening side effects.

If you really want to go deeper, it is the time to start thinking about using boosters that will definitely help in reaching your targeted goal.

Amino Acids

Whey Protein – As you already know by now, your body needs at least a gram of protein for each pound of your weight on a daily basis. This increases your muscle growth and strength and also will prevent deterioration by stopping your body from losing lean mass. The best quality of proteins you can get include:

- **Lactalbumin** from concentrate from whey protein, egg albumin (egg white) poultry, fish, meat, and casein (milk)
- **Vegetable protein** (but not as high in quality as lactalbumin) and soy protein

The right high-quality protein will optimize healthy muscle mass and lean tissue, and will also help in preventing bone and muscle damage associated with weight training. In addition, it increases fat loss, boosts metabolism, and promotes minimized muscle soreness and a shorter recovery time.

Glutamine – The amplest amino acid in your body, it covers more than half of all amino acids in muscle cells. It will enhance exercise performance and stamina. With regular glutamine intake, the usual pains and aches that come after exercise are significantly reduced. You should take 6,000-18,000 mg each day in capsule or powdered form before going to bed or after workouts.

Arginine – This important amino acid is not just great for bodybuilding, but for all sports, because it increases performance. It works by increasing the release of different hormones, even the growth hormone, which will help in increasing and healing your muscles and reducing fat. Our bodies use arginine to create nitric oxide, a chemical that relaxes the muscles around the arteries, which increases tissue oxygenation and blood flow. Take 6,000-12, 000 mg each day.

Ornithine – Just like arginine, ornithine helps in releasing the growth hormone. In addition, it boosts the immune system and also promotes healthy liver regeneration and function by detoxifying ammonia. It is used for bodybuilding because it improves wound healing and performance. Ake 3,000 – 6,000 mg daily.

Valine, Isoleucine, and Leucine – These are known as the branched-chain amino acids since they have a common structure. These three make up 1/3 of all amino acids in muscle cells. You can get them from protein and they are important for mental alertness and vigor, maintaining calm, blood sugar levels and muscle repair and co-ordination. They should be taken as follows: 1,500-6,00mg leucine, 800 – 3,000mg isoleucine and valine each day in divided doses.

Other Natural Busters

Creatine Monohydrate – It has been so hard to keep up with the news about this supplement because it has been under unwanted criticism, political debate and too much moralizing. However, one thing is for sure, it is not a steroid! It is found in our bodies. It is tasteless, natural, and safe and it can be found in protein from animals.

Creatine monohydrate is very popular among bodybuilders because it gives them 5-10 lb. more muscle since it attracts water. Don't confuse it with the kind of fluid retention and bloating caused by congested organs, allergies, or other problems because in these cases, fluid is build up outside the muscles. This booster also neutralizes dangerous free radicals that can be produced when doing heavy exercises.

The daily dosage of creatine is 20gr each day or 0.3 grams per one kg of your weight. After 5 days, you will switch to 0.003 per one kilo to maintain it. Don't forget to drink a lot of water (at least 64 ounces) each day when taking your creatine.

Bovine Colostrum – This non-milk secretion is produced by mammalian mothers (all of them) in the first 48 hours after delivery. This can be a bodybuilder's best friend because it contains many different complex proteins that aid muscle building like the growth and other hormones. This will increase athletic prowess. The dosage is 4-6 capsules of 500mg each day taken on an empty stomach.

Chrysin – This is an extract from passiflora coerulea. How does it help? It boosts testosterone production by even 30% without any conversion into dihydrotestorone or estrogen. This is good because a high level of estrogen can cause fat gain, breast enlargement, and water retention and dihydrotestosterone, which can lead to increased baldness and prostate enlargement. The suggested dosage is 500mg twice a day.

Tribulus Terrestris – This amazing herb is known to be one of the best for bodybuilders. Its incredible effects include increasing the luteinizing hormone, the pituitary hormone responsible for stimulating testosterone. It increases testosterone levels by 30% or even more in just 5 days without any side effects. The benefits you will get are muscle growth and body strength. In addition, this herb promotes faster muscle recovery, increases lean body mass and muscle size, boosts immunity and lowers cholesterol levels, enhances mood, and increases libido. Take 750 – 1, 500 mg each day in divided doses.

Deer Antler Velvet

Pay attention more to this product since it has become popular in the past few years. There are many reasons why and I will get to it shortly. First, I have to tell you one thing. A while ago, it wasn't allowed in sports, and then it was allowed. Then not and now it is acceptable once again. All this fuss because of the main component IGF – 1, an insulin-like growth factor.

IGF-1, growth hormones, and other performance-enhancing drugs were and are still frowned upon in sporting because it is called a way of cheating. Why is it now legal? Because the same IGF-1 is found naturally in food products like milk, eggs, and red meat.

Deer antler velvet is the construction of new antler before it hardens and calcifies. During its growing stage, it is rich in different nutrients and one of them is closely linked to IGF-1, a byproduct produced by its pituitary gland.

Which one is better?

As always, nothing is created equal. Some deer antler velvet products will bring more benefits while some not so much. It is not just because of its form but also its ingredients.

For instance, the various capsules and pills may provide you with a lot fewer IGF-1 benefits because growth hormone is very sensitive to the digestive process. However, there are some other ingredients that can be combined with the growth factor like green tea extract, tribulus terrestris, and other ingredients with an herbal base that help support the pituitary gland.

The best products come in the form of drops and sprays. This is because they dissolve in your mouth and do not go in the gastrointestinal tract. I am not saying that these capsules and pills are not good, but they might give you fewer benefits, all depending upon the ingredients used.

Here are some other benefits you will get aside from increased strength, fat loss, and muscle gain:

- Anti-aging
- Better mental health
- Development of the skeletal system

- Stimulation of the immune system
- Better sex life
- Reduced inflammation
- Better muscle recovery
- Improvement in joint mobility and flexibility
- Increased energy and endurance
- Reduced blood pressure
- Increase in blood circulation and supply
- Improved general health

Dosage

Capsules:

- 1000mg for general health
- 2000mg for therapeutic effect
- 300 mg for increased workout performance

Spray:

There are different dosages for the spray form depending on the manufacturer, which is why you should read the directions before using the product. Just make sure that you hold it in your mouth for 20 seconds so that it can be absorbed.

Bonus Chapter

Simple, Delicious and Effective Pre and Post-Workout Smoothies

Pre-workout Smoothies

A protein-rich smoothie before you start your training will keep you healthy and strong. Not just because of the protein, these shakes are also designed to give you all of the important nutrients you need to increase your testosterone to a good level that will help build muscles.

Blueberry Smoothie

Nutritional Value			
12g Fat	54g Carbs	49g Protein	514 Calories

Ingredients:

- 1 cup blueberries, frozen
- 1 ¼ cups of almond milk, vanilla and unsweetened
- ¼ cup od oats, old-fashioned
- 2 scoops of egg white or vanilla protein powder
- 3 tbsp. of acai powder
- 2 tsp. light nectar

Directions:

1. Combine all ingredients in a blender and blend until very smooth.
2. Drink about 30-60 minutes before training.

Black Smoothies

Nutritional Value			
7g Fat	43g Carbs	49g Protein	405 Calories

Ingredients:

- 1 ½ cup of cherries, frozen
- 1 cup of spinach leaves
- 1 cup of almond milk, chocolate
- 2 scoops of whey protein or egg white powder

Directions:

1. Combine all ingredients and blend them until smooth.
2. Drink about 1 hour before training.

Grapefruit Smoothie

Nutritional Value			
3g Fat	61g Carbs	47g Protein	433 Calories

Ingredients:

- 2 cups of frozen strawberries
- 1 cup juice of pink grapefruit
- 1/3 cup of lime juice
- 2 scoops of egg-white or vanilla whey protein powder
- 5 ice cubes

Directions:

1. Blend all ingredients on high until smooth.
2. Serve 40-60 minutes before training.

Peanut Butter Smoothie

Nutritional Value			
20g Fat	35g Carbs	31g Protein	422 Calories

Ingredients:

- 1 cup of strawberries, frozen
- 3 ice cubes
- 2 tbsp. peanut butter
- 1 tbsp. 100% strawberry fruit spread
- ¾ cup of vanilla almond milk, unsweetened

Directions:

1. Combine all ingredients and blend until smooth.

2. Serve 1 hour before training or use it as a meal replacement.

Post-workout Smoothies

Why are post-workout smoothies important? Because they will speed up the process of recovery, provide essential nutrients, and keep you healthy and energized.

Pineapple Smoothie

Nutritional Value			
8g Fat	59g Carbs	46 Proteins	467 Calories

Ingredients:

- 1 ½ cups of pineapple, frozen
- 5 ice cubes
- ½ fresh orange juice
- ¼ cup pomegranate juice, 100%
- 2 scoops egg-white or vanilla whey protein powder

Directions:

1. Combine the ingredients and blend well until smooth.
2. Serve right after training.

Peach Smoothie

Nutritional Value			
3g Fat	49g Carbs	52g Protein	430 Calories

Ingredients:

- 2 cups of peaches
- ¼ cup of Greek yogurt, fat-free
- ½ cup fresh orange juice
- 2 scoops egg-white or vanilla whey protein powder

Directions:

1. Combine the ingredients in a blender and blend until smooth.
2. Drink after training.

Mango Smoothie

Nutritional Value			
12g Fat	80g Carbs	12g Protein	364 Calories

Ingredients:

- 2 cups spinach
- 1 cup mango frozen
- ½ cup baby carrots
- ½ cup coconut water
- ¼ cup fresh orange juice
- 2 mandarin oranges
- ½ cup plain yogurt

Directions:

1. Blend the ingredients until very smooth.
2. Serve 30-60 minutes after workout.

Beet Smoothie

Nutritional Value			
8g Fat	53g Carbs	18g Protein	332 Calories

Ingredients:

- 1 cup silken tofu
- ½ cup frozen or fresh cranberries
- ½ beet, raw
- 1 small Persian cucumber, peeled
- 1 celery stalk
- 1 cup kale
- 1 orange or ½ cup fresh orange juice
- 2 tsp. honey

Directions:

1. Combine the ingredients and blend on high until very smooth.
2. Serve 40-60 minutes after workout.

Conclusion

Now you have everything you need to start your new life of bodybuilding. As you can see, with proper guidance and information, you can dive into bodybuilding waters without any hassles at all.

Start changing your diet by cleaning your kitchen and ridding it of all the food that is against a good bodybuilding diet; then stock it with what you really need. Don't let the food you have at home become a liability. Don't forget to always keep in mind the principles in this book, because without them, the training won't work and your valuable time will be spent for nothing.

Next, you should choose the type of bodybuilding program you want to follow and start it. Make sure you have your pre- and post-workout smoothie ready because it is what will give you all the energy you need to perform your exercises and it will also help you recover faster. Of course, health is the priority; and with smoothies and your new diet, you will have it in no time at all.

Stop ignoring hormones and start to count them as a primary thing. Increase them to get the maximum muscle gain and also to increase your emotional and physical health. All you need to do is follow the above information and buy the food that is required. In addition, the actual exercises will also help in increasing the right hormones, which means you will get benefits from every side of the bodybuilding life style.

Enjoy your newly-chosen goal and stay strong. Don't rush and be patient, because success won't come if you accelerate things prematurely but only if you work on them and wait for the results of your efforts.

Lastly, if you really enjoyed reading the book, please take time out to share your insights by posting a review on Amazon. It'd be really appreciated.

Thank you and good luck!
Kevin

Made in the USA
Las Vegas, NV
01 July 2023

74107822R00066